OUR FAMILY Memories 2021

BOOK 2 OF 2: JOHN'S TRAVEL PICS

A poignant personal photograph solidifies and enriches a particular memory within our mind — which causes us to recall where we were and what we were doing at a particular time and place in the universe — which, in turn, makes our life a smidge more memorable, meaningful, and magnificent.

This book contains photos mostly derived from John's travels, which mainly comprised bike rides but also some walks and trips.
For photos of family activities, see *Book 1: Family Activities.*

The photos in this book are in chronological order by month and also, for the most part, by date and time. All the photos were taken in Michigan, and over half were taken within a 20-mile radius of the photographer's home. ~ About twenty of the photos also appear in Book 1, so if a photo looks familiar, that's probably why. ~ Lastly, above each photo is a number. It's for identifying the photo in the book-creation process. This number is of no use to the reader.

Contents

January 5

February 10

March 12

April 14

May 24

June 39

July 52

August 83

September 106

October 115

November 124

December 127

Our Family Memories 2021 Book 2 of 2: John's Travel Pics
ISBN: 978-1-938001-89-5
Version: Cover 2022-01-03(2) | Text 2022-01-03(4)

Author/Photographer: John Correll
Publisher: Fulfillment Press
Copyright © 2022 by John Correll. All rights reserved.

Special thanks to friend Dr. Bill Bacheler: For introducing me to the joy of photography while on our one-week bike tour in 2009

Special thanks to entomologist friend Dr. Jack Bacheler: For expert identification of the many insect photos

This book is dedicated to grandson Liam — May you strive always to become the finest person you're capable of being and to create the most beneficial life you're capable of creating ... and, as a result, derive Peace, Love, Joy, and Fulfillment throughout your life.

Beauty of the Seasons

The Beauty of Spring comes from *MOVEMENT*.

The Beauty of Summer comes from V · I · S · T · A.

The Beauty of Autumn comes from **COLOR**.

The Beauty of Winter comes from **STRUCTURE**.

Spring, Summer, Autumn, Winter ...

bring me **Hope**,

           Perspective,

                      Wonder,

                                  Faith.

One of my favorite poems is *The Red Wheelbarrow* by William Carlos Williams, published in 1939. It's heralded by many as being one of the poetry masterpieces of the 20th century. This is it:

**so much depends
upon**

**a red wheel
barrow**

**glazed with rain
water**

**beside the white
chickens**

In the process of creating this book you're now reading I was inspired to create a "follow-up" to that insightful poem. Here it is:

**so much depends
upon**

    seeing

**the red wheel
barrow<u>s</u>**

**glazed with rain
water**

**beside the white
chickens**

The title of the poem is: *Seeing*

JANUARY

843 — Photograph captured along the I-275 bike path in Wayne County, Michigan

"It's the start of 2021 — it's going to be a <u>photogenic</u> year."

853 — expired milkweed pods, along I-275 bike path at I-94 expressway overpass

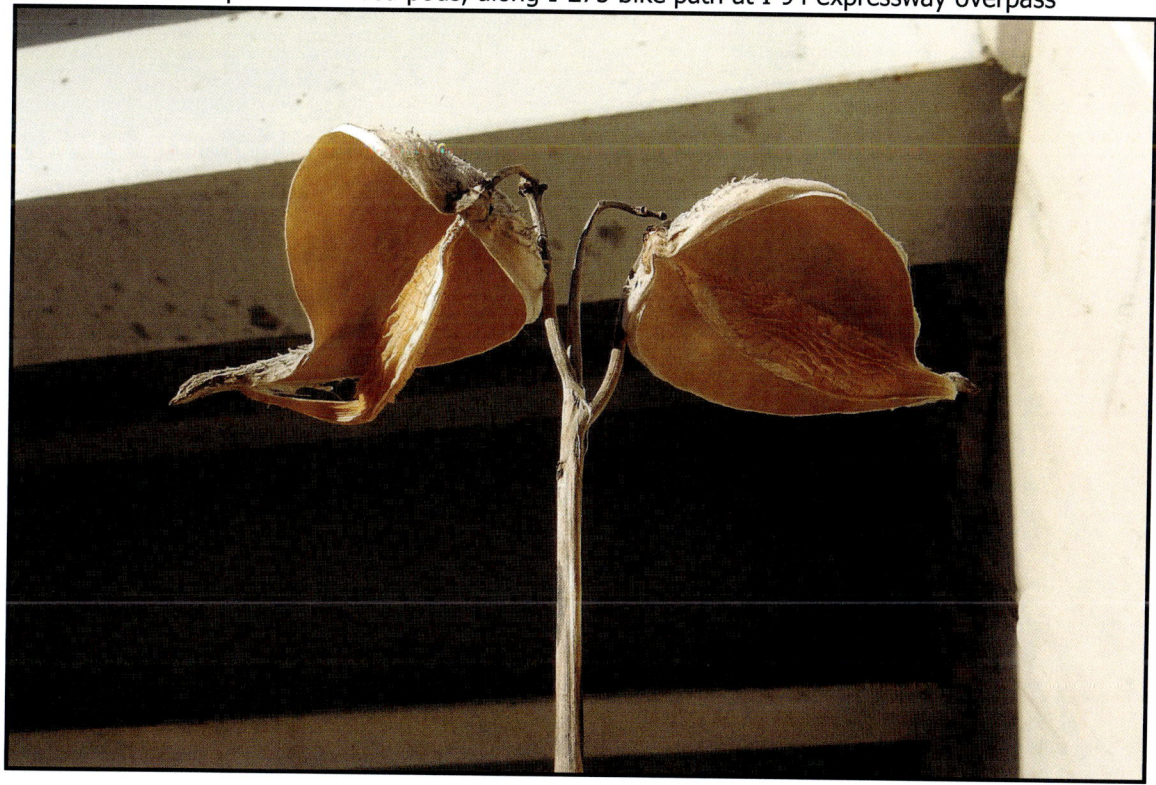

Hanging On

874 — along I-275 bike path at I-94 overpass

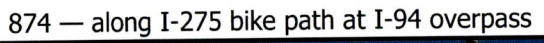

Looking Up

886 — I-275 bike path

To Eternity

"In 1979, I started biking to condition my body.
Then I discovered, my spirit was being conditioned, as well."
— JC

904 — eastward view from my porch, near sundown

Sunset Time

949 — at home

"Good morning — I hope you have a smilin' good day."

952 — view from my front yard

Ghostly Moon

969 — start of a descent, grandson sledding at Hines Park, an 18-mile long park in Wayne County, MI

THE MOMENT — a point of no return

FEBRUARY

993 — post-season holiday decoration on a tree

Wonderland

031 — snowflake on ice

One in a Gazillion

058 — near Ionia, MI

Mystical Moon
(comes once every hundred years, and only in Ionia, Michigan)

MARCH

082 — I-275 bike path

"Been here all winter, waiting for YOU."

129 — left after an accident, next to the I-275 bike path underneath the I-94 overpass

Education for Free
(no government-loan required)

195 — spring flower next to my back deck

"Let spring begin."

143 — Janet at Rite Aid Pharmacy, Ionia, MI

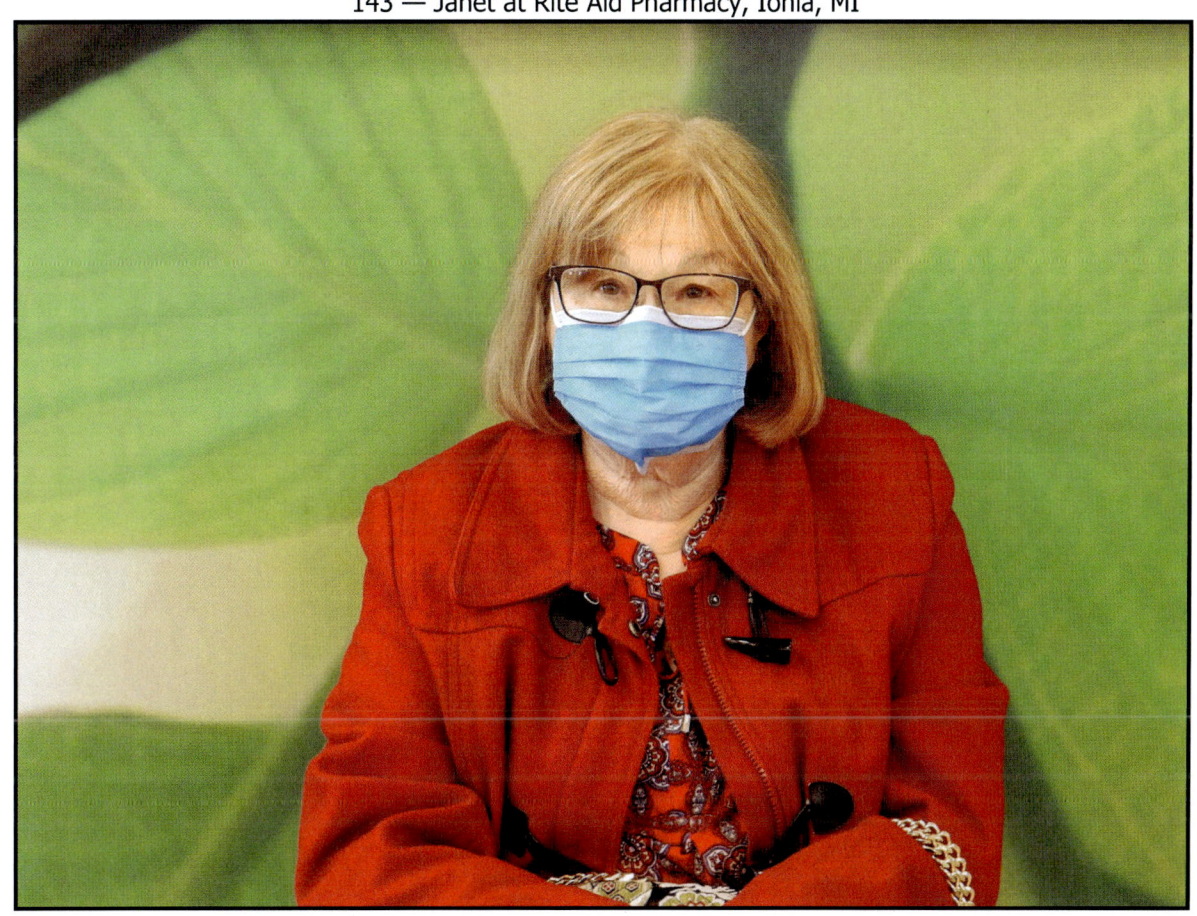

"Free at last — just got my second Covid shot."

APRIL

255 — this photo and the next three were taken at Lake Michigan near Grand Haven

Beach Boy

Month Too Early

259

Cold and Lonely

260 — my favorite of the four beach shots

Trinity

261 — Nunica, MI

"Today old and weathered ... but there was a time, back in the day, when I was not this way. Sometimes I think I may be the only one who remembers."

268 — Nunica, MI

"WHAT are you seeing?"

275 — Nunica, MI

iPod, Boy, and Pet

291 — Nunica, MI

Let There Be Light

April

293 — Nunica, MI

"Come out and play."

306 — Nunica, MI

"What!!!???"

378 — I-275 bike path

Breaking Free

383 — Train track near my home

Never-ending
In the 1800s when railroads began they would say "Rails are forever."
As hyperbolic as that statement seems, it might be it was truer than even they realized.

393 — my front porch

"Which one do you want?"
(I think that perhaps toy vehicles and young boys are made for each other.)

421 — Pair of Muscovy Ducks in Lower Huron Metro Park, during breeding season

Family Time
"Stop your gawking — quick, take your picture and beat it. We have matters to attend to."

427 — Exposed inside surface of a large dead cut-down tree in Lower Huron Metro Park

Red Dead Wood

434 — Lower Huron Metro Park

Spring Has Sprung

473 — groundhog along I-275 bike path

Curious ... and Cautious

506 —my basketball hoop after surprising, rare snowfall in April

"Slam-dunk me, if you can."

MAY

540 — Car keys found by the side of a road while biking (later given to a local Chevy dealership)

Lost & Found

547 — view looking south from Seven Mile Road

Salem Landfill Trash Dump (in the background, a mile away)

551 — located on Seven Mile Road (a mile from the trash dump)

Abandoned — but still home sweet home to somebody

556 — **Turkey Vulture** — He's on top of his home — he and his friends fly a mile to work each day to eat — they're at home right now (see prior photo 551 — look closely)

"Hey, beauty's in the eye of the beholder — right?"

569 — I-275 bike path

Brothers
(male redwing blackbirds)

542 — Seven Mile Road west of Northville

Still Meaningful

574 — horse farm on Seven Mile Road

Pastoral

636 — Author in his driveway

"I've been dreaming for months of beautiful, warm biking season … finally my dream is fulfilled."

684 — Tiny flower on the I-275 bike path (my finger is there to impart size perspective)

The Tiny Team

697 — on I-275 bike path

Tiny Flowers Intrigue

Tiny flowers intrigue me. They're tough to photograph and can often require 10 or 20 takes, but when one finally captures a good photo it can be beautiful and striking. You'll encounter *many more* in this book. My index finger is in most of the photos to provide size perspective. It's also there to focus on, as the camera has trouble focusing on a tiny flower. Plus, on a windy day the finger keeps the flower from "waving in the wind." So, I'm manipulating the flower with my left hand and operating the camera with the right — *very* challenging.

711 — I-275 bike path

Exquisiteness

728 — I-275 bike path

Sunny Side Up

749 — I-275 bike path

"Let's Party."

760 — Whitmore Lake, viewed from a parking lot behind the First Methodist Church

Consecration Time

May

763 — I-275 bike path — a Mallard duck family swimming in the ditch between the expressway and bike path — I frequently encountered them for about a month, then they vanished

"Follow me … and stay in line."

767 — I-275 bike path

Purple Passion

778 — I-275 bike path

"Kiss me."

785 — I-275 bike path

Bursting Forth

807 — I-275 bike path

"I'm beyond tiny — I'm teensy-weensy."

815 — I-275 bike path

Baby Pine Cones
(I believe)

May

835 — new blacktop in a hole in the I-275 bike path

Quite beautiful, for a brief period

840 — I-275 bike path

Breaking Free

870 — I-275 bike path

Monochrome Beauty (green's all we need)

---

886 — I-275 bike path

Singularity

NOTE: I find mushrooms and other fungal life to be fascinating, and great photo subjects. You'll be encountering more in the pages ahead.

888 — Van Born Road where it crosses I-275 bike path

What's this!!?? A giant sheet of aluminum foil hanging from the end of a truck? How'd it get there?

892

Apparently, the truck went under the I-275 Expressway (section above) and the truck was 13-feet and **7½**-inches tall … so the top edge of the truck hit the steel I-beam (at the two shiny spots on the beam) — the truck kept going and the top sheet of the truck didn't, causing it to crinkle up like a piece of fan-folded aluminum foil.

May

899 — I-275 bike path

"Yes, us common clover can be beautiful, too."

908 — I-275 bike path

Sky Bound

897 — I-275 bike path

Summer Glory

932 — a Hummie at Janet's hummingbird feeder — these rascals are challenging subjects to photograph, they're constantly flapping, and seldom stay in one spot more than a couple seconds

Eating on the Fly
(a.k.a., The original Grab-and-Go — OR — the Original Fast-food Eater)

JUNE

967 — I-275 bike path

Going for the Gold
Bumblebee on multiflora rose

993 — I-275 bike path

Small yet Proud

6002 — I-275 bike path

Demure Damsel

---

009 — I-275 bike path

Mystery Beckons

June   40

010 — the ascent of the I-275 bike path where it goes over a train track south of Michigan Ave.

Ascent

019 — Wild Rose — side of I-275 bike path

"Hey, big boy, stop and smell <u>this</u> rose … at least once — before I'm gone."

025 — I-275 bike path

Flowers, woods, pleasant weather and a bike path running through it. Combined with a good bike and health — one can scarcely ask for more.

---

136 — I-275 bike path

Conquering with Numbers
Mites on flower stamens

116 — landfill in Salem Township, MI — four trash bulldozers and one earth bulldozer — these giant landfills are stealthily popping up all over — if we don't get our "trash and garbage thing" figured out soon, someday the planet will be one endless range of trash mountains — and, once each mountain is built it's here for *eternity.*

Everlasting Legacy

It may be that our *trash* will be the lasting legacy of humankind's time on earth — sad, indeed.

151 — I-275 bike path

Breakthrough

121 — I-275 bike path

Monarch Majesty

194 — I-275 bike path

It Rhymes with Orange
(It's orange milkweed — a.k.a. butterflyweed)

157 — This photo and the NEXT ONE were captured while on a walk in Hines Park on **Father's Day**

Connection

162

A good father — and there are many — is a vital asset to a kid, to a community, and to our nation.

186 — I-275 bike path

Plain, Prickly, Stunning
Cutleaf teasel from a prior year's "crop"

192 — I-275 bike path

"It's mine — all mine."
Ant on butterflyweed flowers (a.k.a. orange milkweed)

206 — I-275 expressway viewed from I-275 bike path

Nature and Technology

209 — I-275 bike path

"Join the party."

214 — on I-94, viewed from I-275 bike path

"I'm not actually OUTFRONT, but you get the idea."

218 — I-275 bike path

Battered — but Still Not Beaten

223 — I-275 bike path

Elegante

232 — Several days of downpour caused flooding of the rivers, and also the I-275 bike path. This three-photo sequence shows a "daring biker" traversing a flooded section.

"Well, it can't be THAT deep — I'll go for it."

234

"Ooops."
(On each downstroke his leg is now submerging to the ankle.)

236

"Almost there — oh, well, live and learn."

237 — my neighborhood

Rooftop Lookout

238 — Author in the hands of a world-class dental hygienist (his daughter)

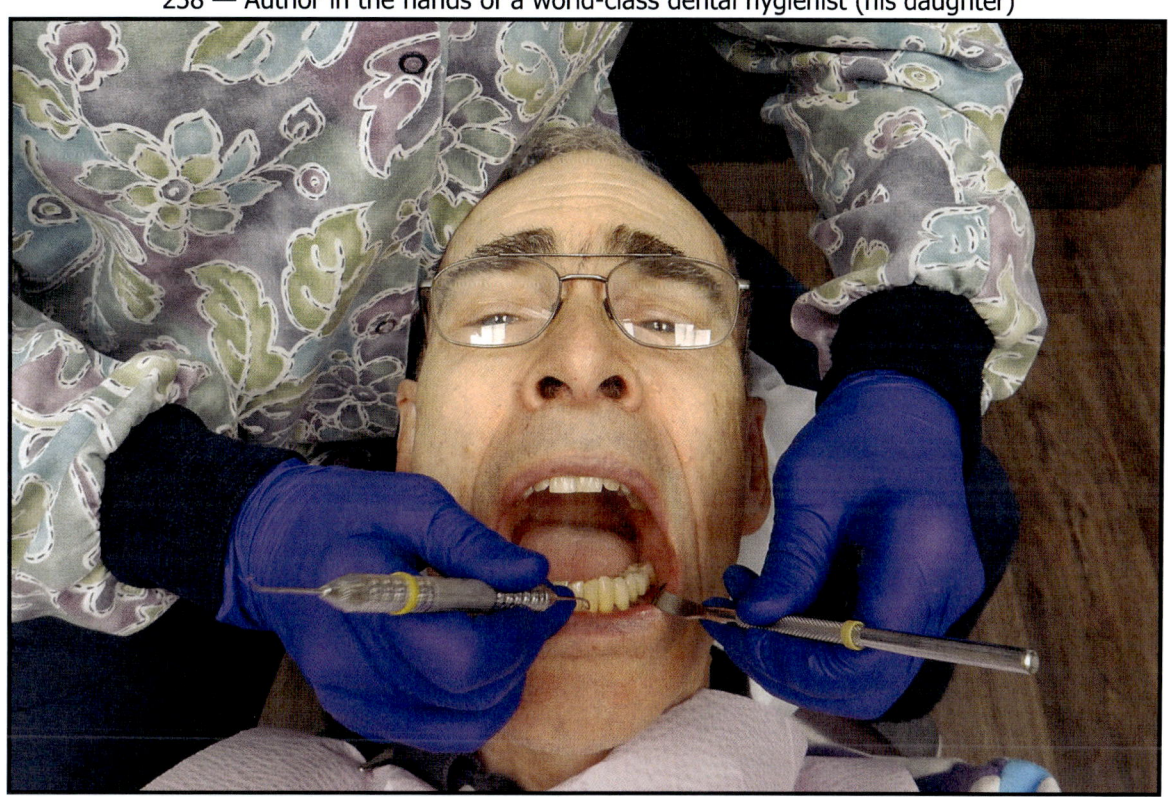

"I hate looking at selfies, and I hate taking selfies. But to capture this unique moment I had no choice."

JULY

244 — **Fritillaria** (I believe it is) in the weeds along the I-275 bike path, a quarter mile south of Ecorse Road

Summer Surprise

245

Beauty in Multifarious Manifestation

254

Heaven Bound

331 — photographed from my back deck

Telecommunications Engineer

342 — photographed from my deck

Cuteness in Blue

273 — I-275 bike path

"No spider am I."
Daddy longlegs (a.k.a. harvestman)

282 — I-275 bike path

"See my proboscis, or 'food tube,' it's longer than my body."
Skipper butterfly on swamp milkweed

283 — I-275 bike path

Surfeit of Plenty
Bumblebee on swamp milkweed
(As you've probably already discerned, the bees and butterflies LOVE this plant species.)

289 — I-275 bike path

"Get in line … or lose out."

306 — I-275 bike path

"It's my home — it's small, but it's MINE."
(I know the sentiment.)
Crab spider on swamp milkweed

369 — I-275 bike path

Weed and Wheels

375 — in the countryside

Marion, the Proud Marine

383 — I-275 bike path

**Steel versus Nature — OR — Manmade versus Wild — OR —
Metal versus Wood — OR — Non-life versus Life**

Which is stronger? Which will prevail?

Look closely, and apply a little imagination, and you can see that the tree has a face: consisting of a mouth, which is holding the fence, a stub-nose above the mouth, and a squinting eye to the right of the nose.

Would you believe, I've been walking and biking past this fence for over 40 years, and had not noticed the unique situation shown above until this day: July 4, 2021.

384 — nearby neighborhood

July 4th and Happy to Be Here

385 — Collection of objects found on one bike ride traversing city and country

Bike Ride Treasure
(the prior owner of the wrench having the nickname "Catfish)

388 — I-275 bike path

Golden Glory

July

394 — I-275 bike path

Creamsicle

404 — I-275 bike path

Pink Passion

408 — I-275 bike path

Shapely

409 — I-275 bike path

Bud and Flower

411 — I-275 expressway viewed from bike path

New-age Rest Stop

423 — Legendary Lafayette Coney Island (downtown Detroit) — established 1914

Keepin' It Clean

424 — Menu Board at Lafayette Coney Island (downtown Detroit)

Proven
(since 1914)

453 — I-275 bike path

Sharing the Feast
Bumblebee and sweat bee on common buttonbush

460 — I-275 bike path

It's the Berries

462 — I-275 bike path

Rugged Beauty

491 — I-275 bike path

Forever

---

496 — hanging on our refrigerator

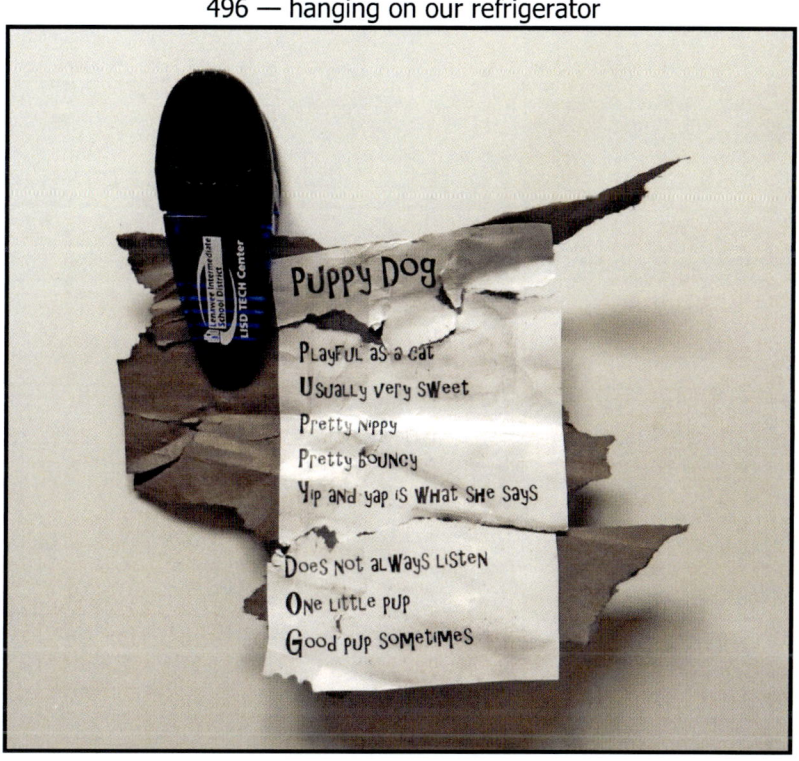

Ode to a Pet

My grandson's fifth grade teacher instructed students to write a poem about a pet. He wrote a poem about his miniature schnauzer puppy. Then he brought it home — and the puppy tried to eat it. (Ironically, the poem's last line is: *Good pup sometimes.*)

All Mine
Bumblebee on cutleaf teasel
In creating this photo I happened to be aiming the camera in the direction of the expressway.
I coincidentally pressed the shutter button exactly when a blue car was passing by.
It made for a surprisingly nice background in the photo.

502 — I-275 bike path

Busy as a Bee
Bumblebee on cutleaf teasel

539 — my backyard

Monarch in the Coneflower Patch

551 — I-275 bike path

Self-possession

554 — I-275 bike path

Parental Care

555 — I-275 bike path

Pink It Is

558 — I-275 bike path

Hanging Out

568 — young Great Blue Heron in Middle Rouge River at Hines Park

Smoothness & Stealth
(If you're a small fish, this gentle-moving avian creature is Death in Disguise.)

571 — I-275 bike path

Adolescent Pine Cone

572 — I-275 bike path

Bloomin' 'Shroom

575 — on Ann Arbor Trail (road)

Roadside Attraction
Sumac bush

July

579 — I-275 bike path

Decision Time

582 — I-275 bike path

Yellow and Gold

July

583 — I-275 bike path

Looking Up

584 — I-275 bike path

"Join the Party."

601 — I-275 bike path

Jewel on a Leaf
(Tortoise beetle is its real name)

618 — I-275 bike path

Butterfly and Bouquet
Checkerspot butterfly on swamp milkweed

630 — I-275 bike path

Looking Tough
Bumblebee on swamp milkweed

---

634 — I-275 bike path

Hungry
Female spicebush swallowtail on cutleaf teasel

663 — I-275 bike path

Butterflies and bees LOVE cutleaf teasel

671 — I-275 bike path

Duo of Young Whitetail Bucks

July

683 — I-275 bike path

Individualist

671 — view from I-275 bike path where it overpasses a train track

"Oh my, what now? Mama warned me of this — dare I venture to the other side of the track?"

734

Ultimate Victory

694 — I-275 bike path

Cruising In
Giant swallowtail on cutleaf teasel

695 — I-275 bike path

Taking Hold
Giant swallowtail on cutleaf teasel

706 — I-275 bike path

Landing
Giant swallowtail on cutleaf teasel

707 — I-275 bike path

Elegant Precision
Giant swallowtail on cutleaf teasel

745 — I-75 Expressway heading north

Michigan Summer Northbound

759 — Jordan River delta just before it enters Lake Charlevoix

Water and Woods (What Michigan Up-north is about)

812 — photo taken at 9:20 a.m. from a dock on the north end of Lake Charlevoix

Morning Exercise

July

823 — one of the many scenic roads in the northern sector of Michigan's lower peninsula

Drive On … and On

---

833 — ultra-sanitary toilet encountered in a gas station restroom

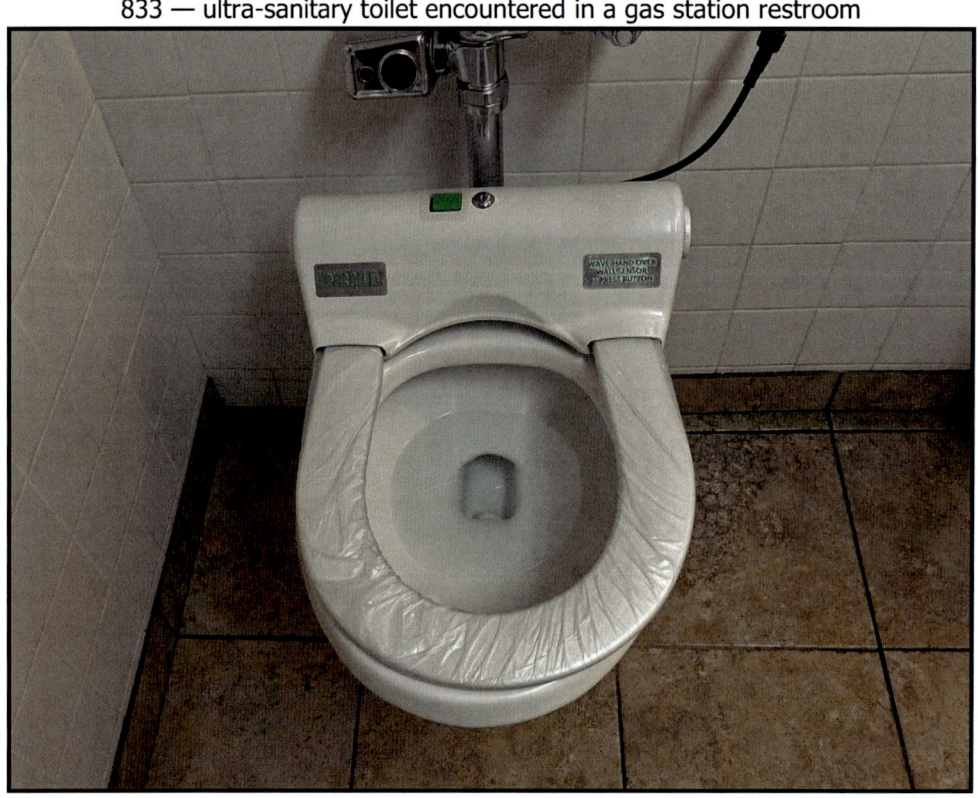

High-tech for the Tush

Press a button and the plastic wrap automatically moves circularly around the seat to "take in" the previously used portion, which then "brings out" a new unused portion.

AUGUST

844 — I-275 bike path

"Whew — sometimes life can be such a whirl."

851 — I-275 bike path

Shelf fungus, I believe it is, on a stump (looks like a bakery treat)

855 — I-275 bike path

No color, no flower — but striking nonetheless

857 — I-275 bike path

Yum!
Carpenter bee on swamp milkweed

August

859 — I-275 bike path

How Sweet It Is
European honeybee on swamp milkweed

865 — I-275 bike path

Nature's Bouquet
Swamp milkweed with its flower blossom in various stages of blooming —
makes for a striking bouquet effect — bees, butterflies, and other insects find it compellingly attractive … and I do, too.

869 — I-275 bike path

Wicked Mystery
Blue mud dauber wasp on swamp milkweed — Does it sting or does it not?
It can sting but seldom stings humans.

870 — I-275 bike path

The Plunge
Japanese beetle on morning glory flower

877 — I-275 bike path

Mid-afternoon Snack
European honeybee on cutleaf teasel

892 — I-275 bike path

Closing In
Giant swallowtail on cutleaf teasel

893 — I-275 bike path

The Ultimate Camouflage — Transparency
Male twelve-spotted skimmer dragonfly

894 — I-275 bike path

Beaten and battered, but still getting it done.
Male eastern tiger swallowtail butterfly on cutleaf teasel

900 — I-275 bike path

Mouthy Young Jay
(Aren't they all?)

Blue jays are tricky to photograph. They're wary and keep their distance, and seldom sit in one spot for long. This one, to my surprise, landed on the fence next to the bike path as I was pedaling along. After passing it, I slowly stopped, then pulled out my camera and snapped this pic. A second later it flew. I was surprised it sat as long as it did.

918 — I-275 bike path

Orange Barrel Graveyard

921 — Lower Huron Metro Park

"The gang's all here."

925 — Lower Huron Metropark

Individuality

926 — I-275 bike path

THE LESSON? Be different, and also in the right place at the right time, and you can be a *standout*.

---

928 — I-275 bike path

Looking Tough
Late-blooming Milkweed Pods

932 — I-275 bike path

"When you got THE SHAPE you don't need gaudy color."

940 — I-275 bike path

Middle of the Road

Many persons view it as being the easy, copout life. But, truth is, it ain't easy — and it's not a copout. Retreating to one side or the other and hiding in a crowd of like minds is the copout.

August

949 — I-275 bike path

Space Satellite

994 — this photo and the next five were taken on the south shore of Beaver Island (in Lake Michigan)

Serenity

7015 — Beaver Island,. south shoreline

Beach in Early Morn

021 — Beaver Island

Hanging Out

022 — Beaver Island

In the Sands of Time

027 — Beaver Island

For a Few Seconds Only

033 — Beaver Island

Water, Wave, Sand, Pebbles

096 — I-275 bike path

It's the Glide
Male black swallowtail

097 — I-275 bike path

Perfect Landing
Male black swallowtail on annual ragweed

101 — I-275 bike path

Pampas Grass Glory
It's in autumn that the top tassel on pampas grass blooms, and waves gloriously in the wind for the rest of the year.

August

107 — I-275 bike path

Family Reunion
Aphids on milkweed seed pod

242 — I-275 bike path

Purple and Orange
Monarch butterfly on purple loosestrife

273 — I-275 bike path

Dangerously Incautious

316 — I-275 bike path

Petite Pink Perfection

224 — Nunica, MI

Peek-a-moon

238 — at my home

Sinister Sun

August

Two Minutes in August
(in Six Photos)

Around 3:15 p.m. on Wednesday, August 4, I was biking northbound on the I-275 bike path and approaching the Ford Road intersection. It was a hot, sunny-bright day. As I was crossing the intersection at Ford Road a high-speed police cruiser — siren wailing, lights flashing — sped north up the expressway. Then, from various directions — one after another — more frantic police cruisers converged on an area on the expressway several hundred yards north of Ford Road. Then a monster, wailing fire truck came, followed by an ambulance.

Anxious to see what the excitement was about I quickened my pace. Within a minute I was at the scene. I parked my bike, pulled out my camera, and — from my position on the bike path — began taking photos. Here are six pics conveying what I saw during a span of about two minutes.

903 — I-275 Expressway, northbound — **3:20 p.m.**

A car is upside down in the median. Expressway traffic has been halted. Multiple police and firefighters are on the scene. They're focused on what's inside an overturned vehicle. There are no other cars. So it wasn't a multi-car accident. I pondered how this vehicle could have overturned. I conjectured that the driver fell asleep (it was a bright, hot day) and drifted off the highway and into the culvert in the median — then flipped.

905 — **3:20 p.m.**

With my camera I zoomed in for a closer view. It became apparent that two men were on their knees, desperately attempting to "make contact" with someone in the vehicle. One man was a firefighter, in a tan jacket. The other man was wearing a medium blue jumpsuit — I couldn't ascertain whether he was connected to the police or to the firefighting unit, or maybe he was a motorist driving close behind the accident and stopped to help and was the first person on the scene. After about 30 seconds, the man in the jumpsuit appeared to try to crawl-and-squeeze through a window space. He got about halfway into the car.

907 — **3:21 p.m.**

Then the man in the jumpsuit (shown above) emerged from the overturned car. The two men stood up. No longer were they focusing attention on what was inside the mangled vehicle. Some of the other men stepped closer.

(Note: The reason this photo and the next one are blurry is because the auto-focus feature on my camera was focusing on the reeds in the foreground, and I didn't realize it at the time.)

908 — **3:21 p.m.**

Then a couple of the other men began focusing on the man in the jumpsuit who had squeezed partway into the car. And they began talking to him and making what appeared to me to be "understanding" gestures. I don't know for certain what the situation was that precipitated this, but it didn't appear to be a happy one. Your conjecture is as good as mine.

909 — **3:22 p.m.**

For some reason, a second fire truck came wailing to the scene. But there's no longer commotion or excitement — indeed, no apparent reason for it to be there. The police officers continued talking to the man in the jumpsuit, as if to say, "You did all you could — sometimes you just can't save a sad situation."

910 — **3:22 p.m.**

Then the men dispersed from the area of the overturned car. Police began setting up a lane for the backed-up expressway traffic to begin moving past in single file. I put my camera away, hopped onto my bike, and headed for home — still wondering how it happened that that car overturned …
and who was the person inside it.

SEPTEMBER

332 — I-275 bike path — Great White Egret in a tree

"White can be a beautiful 'color' too."

418 — I-275 bike path

*"So, in your opinion, what's the most beautiful:
a captivating COLOR or a striking SHAPE?"*

421 — I-275 bike path

"Sometimes captivating color combined with striking shape can be bomb."

---

433 — I-275 bike path

"And, a collage of a single shape and one color can be eye-catching, too."

431 — I-275 bike path

Purple and Gold — seems like the colors of a college sports team

446 — my neighborhood

"Oh, my gosh — WHAT am I doing here?"

(NOTE: September–October is when mushrooms and other fungi come into their glory.)

477 — I-275 bike path

TOP view of shelf fungus on a tree in a woods

493 — I-275 bike path

BOTTOM view of a giant shelf fungus on a dead tree by the bike path
(Interestingly, when I biked by this spot just three days later expecting to revisit this magnificent fungus, it was gone — someone had sawed down the tree. It was a smidge saddening.)

518 — I-275 bike path

Golden Glory

539 — I-275 bike path

Classic "Toadstool"

541 — I-275 bike path

One of the captivating things about mushrooms is their unique shapes.

542 — I-275 bike path

"Let's dance."
(Two shapes in one pic)

Wings and Wires

A Few Seconds in September

Now, let me share with you a story you might, at first, not believe. See that horizontal fallen tree in the photo, the one extending all the way across the bike path? At 12:04 p.m. on Friday, September 24, I rode smack-dab *right into it.* Nothing close to that has ever happened to me before ... and I hope nothing like it ever happens again. It went like this.

As you can see from the photo, it was a sunny, balmy afternoon. I was blithely cruising southbound down the I-275 bike path on my 2-wheeler at about 10–12 miles per hour. I don't know where I was looking at the time, but I know for certain it was NOT at the path ahead. Maybe I was looking at the woods, or at expressway traffic, or at a billboard, or at the clouds, or — perhaps most likely — at the foliage on the right side of the path, in the area between the path and the expressway. Suddenly, out of the corner of my eye, I spotted that tree in front of me. Unfortunately, I was only about *four feet* from it. That's about one second away. I couldn't turn the bike, or grab the brakes, or do anything except HIT the tree straight on. I do recall that in that moment the thought that shot through my brain was **"Oh, shit!!!"**

So I crashed into that tree straight on. Amazingly — or perhaps, miraculously — the height of the tree was such that my bike went *underneath* it and the tree hit me at the best possible height: it struck me across the chest at the height of my armpits. If it had hit me a few inches lower it would have smashed against my solar plexus or ribs and surely broken some bones. Or, it would have caught the bike handlebars, which would have instantly stopped the bike and sent me hurtling *headfirst* over the handlebars and tree. OR, if it had hit me a few inches higher it would have caught me in the neck. Which would have either snapped my neck or, at the least, condemned me to an extended hospital stay. So, the tree hit me — or, more correctly, I hit the tree — at the best possible place: across the chest at armpit level.

When I hit it, my body went from vertical to horizontal in a fraction of a second. Then, in another fraction of a second, I slammed down onto the blacktop on my back, with my head hitting ground at the same time. Fortunately, my helmet cushioned the blow to my skull. For a few seconds my head spun. Then I wondered if I had broken any bones. So I carefully began to get up. I was thrilled to discover that everything seemed okay. So I then went to my bike and picked it up. Amazingly, it too had sustained no damage from hitting the ground. At that point I decided to try to move the tree off the bike path. The tree had a secondary limb that extended diagonally upward into a large bush (in the photo the left end of that limb is now resting on the blacktop). To swing the tree off the path I first needed to free that diagonal limb from the bush (shown on right side of the photo). After a minute or so of yanking and pushing from varying angles the limb surprisingly broke free of the main portion of the tree that I ran into. Yes, I know that limb looks huge and, therefor, unbreakable, but it was fully dead wood and, so, when pulled hard enough it broke free of the main tree.

At that point it occurred to me to capture a photo, which resulted in the above picture. I did this because I realized that without a pic no one would likely ever believe my story or understand what I was talking about. After snapping the photo I then proceeded to try to swing the tree off the bike path. After a minute of pushing and pulling I made progress at it. But I was having difficulty getting it fully to the side and over the fence. Then another biker came along, who stopped and assisted. With team effort we succeeded in swinging the tree entirely off the path and lifting it over the fence.

I then hopped onto my bike and finished the ride, thankful that I was still alive, fully functioning, and able to carry on. I also resolved that I absolutely MUST stay diligently alert to what's ahead, even when I'm biking down a pathway that I've safely traversed hundreds of times over many years. And, lastly, I concluded that in having escaped injury I had received a blessing, so I should commit to making the best of that blessing in my years ahead.

OCTOBER

590 — I-275 bike path

Friendship

597 — I-275 bike path

Meet the Family

636 — I-275 bike path

It's a Pampas Grass Day

656 — I-275 bike path

Circularity
(Snail shell — How does nature dream up designs like this?)

684 — I-275 bike path

Yes, you've seen this scene before, but in a different season (p. 7)

698 — viewed from I-275 bike path, showing intersection of the expressway off-ramp to Ecorse Road

Impending

700 — I-275 bike path

Occasionally a billboard actually *enhances* a scene.

713 — I-275 bike path

Forthcoming

730 — I don't recall where I captured this photo

Near Perfection
(Can you spot the "imperfection?")

735 — I-275 bike path

"And I'm watching you, too."
Chinese praying mantis

762 — off-ramp of I-275 expressway, viewed from the bike path

Autumn Decoration

783
This photo and the next two captured on an autumn color tour in Michigan's thumb region, on a rainy, gray day

Dirt Road between Harvested Fields

791

Nature's Billboard

781 — roadside rest stop next to Lake Huron

Janet is our Trips Navigator — and, in some ways, also my Life Navigator.

804 — view of construction area on I-275 expressway on a Sunday when no one was working

Sunday, Day of Rest

814 — I-275 bike path, in a woods that the path goes through

Autumn Woods Bike Path

819 — view from the I-275 bike path (adjacent an expressway off-ramp)

Don't You Dare!

NOVEMBER

827 — biking/walking path through a woods in Hines Park

Light at the End (or Journey's End)

830 — the Lakeview mountain biking trail in Hines Park

No Matter What

866 — I-275 bike path

Autumn Flowers

878 — first snowfall of the season (my front lawn) — didn't last for long

Melting Beauty

882 — I-275 bike path

Nature's Bed

889 — I-275 bike path

Time to Beat It

A "long shot" at high zoom — this statuesque whitetail deer never stopped keeping me in view, and eventually decided to bolt, which is what it's starting to do here.

DECEMBER

120 — during a walk near home

Spirit of the Season

On December 24, I took a walk in Hines Park (an 18-mile long park in Wayne County, MI). It contains some interesting historic buildings, one which is depicted in the next 4 photos.

109 — the "Haggerty Comfort Station" in Hines Park about 200 yards west of Haggerty Road

Hello, may I be of service?
Erected 1937 — to be a "Comfort Station" for travelers and park visitors

110 — sign in front of the building in the prior photo (109)

A sign in front of the building explains its fascinating history

111 — Enlarged section of the above sign

As the sign explains, this building is an historic forerunner in the world of automotive travel. But you wouldn't know it by looking at it. Today it's minimally used, and stands alone by the side of road.

112 — Enlargement of the photograph contained in the sign (photo 110)

The line of people in the photo is all women. As you might surmise, this line extends from the entrance to the Women's Restroom. (Amazingly, a half-century later architects and building designers are still creating structures having inadequate toilet facilities for ladies.) Also, something else I found interesting is: The racial composition of the line is approximately 50:50 white and black.

167 — Abandoned Rest Stop area on I-275 — now being used by expressway repair workers, who have been working on expressway repair since the prior spring

Road Barrel Hospice

181 — Janet and I took a New Year's Eve drive through the Wayne County Lightfest in Hines Park — this is my favorite of the displays

A bright future awaits — for 2022 and beyond.

Life of a Fungus Family in 14 Pics

In mid-July, while biking on the I-275 bike path, I came upon a unique-looking shelf-type fungus on top of an old tree stump that had been sawed off at ground level. I photographed it (shown below). Five days later, passing it again, I noticed that it looked slightly different from when I had seen it a few days prior. So I captured another photo. I continued doing this for the rest of the year. Following are 14 photos showing how this little family, or colony, of fungi transpired for the remaining six months of 2021. At the top of each photo is the **DATE** of the photograph.

468 — **July 14, 2021**

469 — **July 19**

The small growth in the upper left of the prior photo is growing, as is also the large shiny-reddish growth. The mushroom in the upper right is now gone.

851 — **August 2**

The "small growth in the upper left" is now taking over. And, the shiny-reddish growth is gone (could it be an animal ate it?)

102 — **August 17**

The growth continues growing, and the "cinnamon-looking" center portion is expanding. Note that two small white growths have appeared in lower right.

276 — **August 25**

The large white growth continues growing. The two small ones are bursting forth and have acquired the shiny-reddish brown look of the big growth in the original photos (468, 469).

347 — **September 4**

All the growths appear to be taking on a cinnamon color and texture.

376 — **September 10**

Note that a couple small white growths have appeared above the big one, in the upper right of the photo.

---

475 — **September 18**

Several of the small white growths in the upper right are beginning to grow. And, the prior larger growths are beginning to show "desiccation."

554 — **September 26**

The small growths continue growing.

579 — **September 29**

The larger growths are continuing desiccation; the smaller ones in upper right are continuing to grow.

607 — **October 13**

The ones in upper right are still growing.

749 — **October 28**

The growths in upper right are acquiring a shiny reddish appearance.

850 — **November 7**

All the growths appear to be "expiring" for the season.

024 — **December 2**

The fungus family is now almost entirely gone.
It'll be interesting to see if a new generation emerges next spring in 2022.

so much depends
upon

      seeing

the red wheel
barrow<u>s</u>

glazed with rain
water

beside the white
chickens

Made in the USA
Monee, IL
28 March 2022

08f7b535-3106-44d9-803c-8ebcd4c0e2dcR01